All Scripture references taken from the KJV of the Bible, unless otherwise indicated.

**ANCESTRAL POWERS**, by Dr. Marlene Miles

www.marlenemilestheauthor.com

Freshwater Press, USA,
freshwaterpress9@gmail.com

ISBN: 978-1-960150-50-9

Copyright 2023 by Dr. Marlene Miles

All rights reserved. No part of this book may be reproduced, distributed or transmitted by any means or in any means including photocopying, recording or other electronic or mechanical methods without prior written permission of the publisher except in the case of brief publications or critical reviews.

## Table of Contents

Ancestral Worship ................................................................. 5
What Happens in a Graveyard .......................................... 11
Graveyard Protection Prayer ............................................. 19
Graveyard Witchcraft ......................................................... 22
Soul Tied to Ancestors ....................................................... 24
Ancestral Powers ................................................................ 27
Spitting Image .................................................................... 28
Don't Set the Table ............................................................ 31
Household Wickedness ..................................................... 34
*Familiar Spirits* ................................................................. 37
As A Man Thinketh ............................................................ 40
Strongmen ......................................................................... 43
Monitoring Spirits .............................................................. 47
Enforcers ............................................................................ 49
Family Captivity ................................................................. 51
Tormentors ........................................................................ 52
Killers & Destroyers ........................................................... 54
Guardian Angel vs. Guardian Demon ............................... 58
I've Met A Few ................................................................... 59
Gates & Gatekeepers ........................................................ 60
The Gates of Your Life ....................................................... 64
Possess the Gates .............................................................. 69
Prophesy ............................................................................ 76

| | |
|---|---|
| What's the Name of that Gate? | 81 |
| & A Child Shall Lead Them | 84 |
| Break Free | 89 |
| Other books by this author | 98 |

# ANCESTRAL POWERS

# Ancestral Worship

These days, I hear a lot about ancestral worship. People believe that their ancestors who have transitioned, that is, passed on are watching over them as they continue their current lives here on Earth. Many folks, Catholics especially, believe that their dead relatives have turned into angels and are watching over them. Some Protestants believe that too.

**Humans do not turn into angels.**

Angels are created beings; God created them. God is in His Seventh Day and He has ceased from *creating*. He is at rest, seated in Glory.

Only in movies do angels ever become human. Only in movies do humans ever become angels.

Angels are created to be angels and they remain angels. In the same way, humans are formed and created by God to be humans. God does not turn humans into angels once they are dead, nor do they morph into winged creatures on their own. Ever. Please show me in the Bible where God **ever** did this.

Man is created a little lower than Elohim. Elohim is God. Angels worship God and serve mankind, so are we to think that after dying we are ***demoted***? People who think they are reincarnated into animals and trees think similarly if they think they will come back as some form of mulch, or nature. Wizards, again in the movies, turn people into *things* and creatures, not God.

Ancestral worship is idolatry. Preliterate societies in Africa, China, Korea, Slavic countries, Mayans, and other prehistoric cultures are steeped in ***ancestral worship***. According to what I've seen recently on social media, ancestral worship has staged a comeback as people believe worshipping their ancestors empowers their current life.

Some Americans set a place of "honor" at their dinner tables, especially on holiday occasions for their dead ancestor–, patriarch, matriarch--, whomever. That is a form of ancestral worship, and idolatry. The dead are not coming back to eat. Spirits don't get to come back because you want them to or offer them food and drinks. Spirits don't eat natural food.

Hawaiian culture saturates in ancestral worship as well. Their religion is protected by the American Indian Religious Freedom Act. Everyone can believe and practice their beliefs as they choose, but for Christians, ancestral worship is **not** part of our faith and this practice should not be added to Christianity. No one can get into Heaven, except by Jesus Christ, and Him alone. One cannot add a bunch of religions and deities together, then throw Jesus in to hedge their bets and still get to Heaven.

In a village in Greece, on the Sunday after Easter, the living gather at the cemetery to have lunch with the dead. This is a form of ancestral worship. It is a tradition, and traditions make the Word of God to no effect.

There are numerous old photos of graveyard picnics at St. Luke's in Isle of Wight County just south of Richmond, Virginia. Decoration Day arose by this tradition just after the Civil War, 1868, where people went to adorn graves and have lunch with deceased relatives. Decoration Day was later named Memorial Day.

Day of the Dead is celebrated in Mexico, Guatemala, and other Latin countries where people think they are honoring their deceased friends, and relatives. They build altars, clean gravestones, and prepare food for the living *and* the dead. In Guatemala, building and flying giant kites is a big deal, attracting tourism.

Eating in graveyards had, and still has, historical precedent. People picnic among the dead across the world. Traditions involving eating meals with deceased relatives is a common practice in Asia, too. Americans are not off the hook, they also used to picnic in cemeteries.

Young people, both juvenile and adults, the type who like scary campfire stories, and the macabre, would meet in graveyards for social reasons or as a stupid dare. But even in broad daylight after the Civil War people would get gussied up and take a picnic to the graveyard on an afternoon, to have lunch with the dearly departed. Was this a carryover for the people in the Melting Pot who brought their traditions with them from all over the world? Or were these people in heavy and constant grief because from 1800's to early 1900's people didn't live very long. From the Civil War and even before, children and women were dying in childbirth, there was cholera and other dread diseases. Dr. Fleming didn't discover penicillin until 1928, which changed things, health wise to a large degree.

Lunching in cemeteries was not always cringy, the cemetery turned into the shopping mall Food Court for Victorians; it was the hang out spot. The park-like American cemeteries developed in the mid-1800s and were intended to be recreational areas for people to visit the dead--, and picnic. Before public and national parks became a thing, people would lunch in cemeteries. No kidding. A cemetery in Brooklyn, NY had a no-picnicking posting not because it was a weird thing to do, but mostly because the picknickers trashed the place.

You can probably guess, since families were hanging out with the gravestones and tombs of their deceased relatives, the relative was the focal point of the day. Because of that, it might be easy to fall into worshipping *Grandpa* or whosever gravestone the picnic was held at.

Christians, we don't worship people when they are alive; it is idolatry. That doesn't change when they die, it is still idolatry, and it is ancestral worship. The *spirit of death* is invited into and comes into a family that participates in ancestral worship.

Worship belongs to God.

# What Happens in a Graveyard

What happens in graveyards? Do you really want to know? You need to know. If you are going to a graveyard for any Christian reason, go prayed up. A lot of things can happen there. There can be a transference of *spirits* because it is a dead yard, as my 5-year-old niece used to call them, it attracts living and dead *human spirits, and also non-human spirits*. It's a portal of sorts--, practically a vacation spot--, for a witch.

Witches and those who practice the black arts love graveyards. Graveyard dirt is called *goofer* dust and it is used in the occult. Curses are spoken over graveyard dust, which is used to cast harmful spells on people. It is intended to cause harm, trouble, or even kill an *enemy*. The person casting the spell may believe they are casting against an enemy, but sometimes that perceived enemy is guilty of absolutely nothing against that witch; in that case harm is cast against a *victim.*

Witches or their representatives collecting items to use in spells and rituals, or the actual casting of spells could be happening in a graveyard or cemetery. These could look like normal people, but they are doing some very spiritually wicked and dangerous things.

I know people who are not even *known* to be witches who love funerals. They like the drama. They like the food. In their defense, they get to see people they may not have seen for years up until then. Sad circumstances--, but still.

Teenage pranks, young people in ignorant, spooky dares or hazing may be found in a graveyard. Parents, you should know where your children are and what they are doing at all times. *Thank you.*

Cemeteries can function as portals or gateways to spiritual realms. Jesus said, **Let the dead bury their dead**, so I'm supposing that what's happening in a graveyard ain't of

God, because that verse makes me think that Jesus was not planning to be there.

Roads or pathways that lead to graveyards are called *ley lines* and they are purported to carry a certain energy. Ley lies were described as the ancient roads that funeral processions traveled because it was illegal to **not** take the deceased in a **straight line** to the burial site. These very straight roads used to be called *death roads*. This is from Dutch folklore.

People would avoid crossing or walking on a *death road* because of the high possibility of meeting a *ghost*. Ghost hunter types, and those who observe paranormal activities in graveyards seem to agree such activity is higher in older, broke down, abandoned cemeteries than in newer, well-kept ones. They say disembodied *human spirits* avoid people. See the difference between fallen angels, malevolent entities, and evil *spirits* versus *human spirits*?

These *ghosts* are supposedly more active at night than in the daytime which adds spookiness to witch folklore and juvenile overnight graveyard challenges. It is rumored that they prefer certain weather conditions, certain times of year, such as solstices, Halloween, and the crescent moon. Pagans usually have their holidays around these thinly veiled times where *spirit* activity might be higher.

Those who can see in the spirit might see spirits as mists, for example. Of course, a mist, could arise from warm soil when the air is colder. Mulch steams because it is warmer than the air around it. Ever notice that?

I'm sharing all this to say that people do believe that the spiritual shells of the deceased hovers around their own gravesite especially if they are still earthbound, still attached to their earthly life and can't let go--, as if this is an option. Those who die in Christ are not earthbound or otherwise tied up by the underworld. An angel of the Lord should come and escort a saved person to their eternal destination.

So, family members who come to gravesites to mourn **repeatedly**, allegedly pull these *spirits* back to the Earth realm. People say, **Rest in Peace**, but in excessive mourning, they are compelling lost souls and earthbound spirits to linger at the site where grieving is most intense, but they are rarely visible except by those who can see in the spirit.

There are occultists, such as witches, who frequent cemeteries and also those who work for occultists who go and fetch things for evil human agents to use in their witchcraft such as *goofer* dust as we have previously mentioned. Believe me, they are sent for worse and more mind-boggling things and purposes than just dirt.

There are also dark or malevolent spiritual entities that frequent cemeteries, including those that feed off the *emotions* of mourners who come repeatedly to the burial site. The devil loves trauma because he can use that. Grief is trauma. Grief opens the door for the devil to allow other evil *spirits* to enter a person's life. Often the **person thinks they are talking to the deceased or some other ancestral person in their family,** but no *human* spirit is there. It's a demon. Or more than one demon.

Some time ago, when visiting the Catacombs in Rome, it was pointed out by the tour guide that Christians were buried and pagans were cremated. Kind of makes one *think*-- when there are grave robbers and folks who don't mind desecrating a grave...

Wherever you go, especially to a cemetery be tuned in. If you feel strange when visiting a graveyard, it could be that you are a very spiritually sensitive person, but it could be because the site is host to a multitude of *spirit* beings. For instance, you may experience goose bumps or a chill. If you feel a drop in your stomach, this may be a warning sign that you have entered a place frequented by powerful and possibly malevolent entities.

Practice discernment so when you feel something spiritual, you know what that spiritual feeling is and where it is coming from. If you are spiritually sensitive but have not *discerned* the source of the things you feel, being at a gravesite of a loved one and feeling *feels*, may make you think you are feeling that departed person, when it could be something else entirely. Some other entity could be *impersonating* your dear one. It could know that you will *feel* it, but you won't know where it's coming from so you will accept it.

Lots of things are spiritual, but everything spiritual is not good, or of God.

*Guardian spirits, and territorial spirits* can hover and watch over cemeteries, churches, monuments, old battlefields, and ancient temple ruins.

While in the Holy Land, visiting the Tomb that Jesus was to have been lain after His crucifixion I noticed the intense energy of that spot. Instantly I knew I had to discern is this **Jesus energy** or is this the energy of the millions of people who have visited this ruins? How can you know? Holy Spirit is the only way to know. Pray.

One would be mistaken to think of cemeteries as spiritual havens. Although they may be tranquil in their physical appearance, there may be all kinds of unpleasant, shadowy things happening there, especially at night.

The jazz funerals of New Orleans began as the people thought that the music would please the *spirits* that watch over the dead. Wow.

If you're going to a graveyard at all, go prayed up.

Observing myths, folklore and old wives tales is NOT being prayed up. One myth is that *standing near an open grave can cure minor aches and pains, such as toothaches;* that is superstition. Don't do it.

# Graveyard Protection Prayer

Lord, thank You that You have not given us the *spirit of fear*, but one of Love, power and a sound mind. I bind up *fear* and all superstition as I go into this graveyard/cemetery, in the Name of Jesus.

Thank You, Lord for Your Spirit is with me, going before me, in me, and You are my rearguard with Goodness and Mercy following after me, so nothing untoward will happen today, in the Name of Jesus.

Help me to behave myself here so there is no temptation to bring anything home knowingly. I will pick up nothing found here, including money.

Lord, let no *human spirit in any condition,* or fallen angelic spirit, their warfare, sin, or corruption transfer to me, in any way, in the Name of Jesus.

I pray that no sin, warfare, corruption, word, judgment, curse, spell, ritual, dedication, sacrifice, hex, vex, jinx, hoodoo, voodoo, sorcery, or other incantation of any kind, from any occultic agent will transfer to me or have any effect on me. I forbid it, in the Name of Jesus. Cover me in the Blood of Jesus.

I bind every *disembodied spirit,* in the Name of Jesus.

I bind every malevolent *spirit,* in the Name of Jesus.

I bind the *spirit of death and the grave* in Jesus' Name.

Lord, cover our footprints, our foot tracks, even our tire tracks with the Blood of Jesus. Father, keep personal items that are left here inadvertently from being used by evil human agents, in the Name of Jesus.

I bind every witch and all forms of witchcraft and forbid any evil from transferring to me or to any other person as a result of being here today, in Jesus' Name.

By the power of Christ Jesus and the Blood of Jesus, no evil altar, seen or unseen will have any effect on me or anyone here, in the Name of Jesus.

I pray the same for the bereaved. Bring Your Peace and Strength to the Family of the deceased. I bind the *spirits of excessive grief, heaviness* and *pining* away, in the Name of Jesus. The joy of the Lord, be their strength and keep them from **ancestral worship.**

Lord, do not let this death, or this life be in vain. Hear every cry of repentance for this soul. Let their soul be in the arms of Abraham, their spirit home with the Lord Jesus Christ. Lord, have Mercy on our deceased friend/loved one, in the Name of Jesus.

Lord, have Mercy on us all; help us walk upright before You all the days of our lives, so that we may be well pleasing to You, in the Name of Jesus,

Amen.

# Graveyard Witchcraft

A cemetery is not just a place of burial of the deceased; everything there is not dead. This place can act as a portal of sorts; witches and those who practice black, green, red or white magic flock to them. To protect yourself be prayed up when you have to go to a funeral or graveyard. Follow these suggestions:

Don't bring anything from a graveyard home such as flowers, even the pretty wild daisy that you want as a keepsake. Those who practice the occult do graveyard rituals and they use what may appear to be normal everyday things. Some of these things are left in the cemetery overnight or even several nights. So you don't know who left what there. Leave it all there.

Ritual items could include food. Definitely do not eat any food you *find* at a graveyard. I'm actually rethinking eating any food at a funeral at all. Other things used in witchcraft rituals are personal belongings, clothes and especially money. Don't touch it; these are favorite ritual items of voodoo and hoodoo priests. These things are used to transfer disease, charms, and spells by those who practice black magic.

Don't play around in a cemetery, especially on a dare. Don't try to do any spells you read about online. You could open up a world of hurt that you may not be able to get out of. That hurt could also pass on to your children and grandchildren, and you won't be able to stop it. For reasons that may or may not be obvious do not allow a picture of a living person to be buried with a deceased person. Because of the possibility of the transference of spirits, pregnant women and small children should not go to cemeteries. It would be best not to take pictures at a cemetery.

Eating and drinking at the graveyard --, we are back to that again? Yup. Picnicking with the deceased. Don't do it.

## Soul Tied to Ancestors

The purpose of the previous chapter is to warn those who are soul tied to ancestors or who are intent on **ancestral worship** to the point of repeatedly visiting, mourning, crying over, worshipping a headstone is that you are treading on spiritually dangerous territory.

*Let the meditation of my heart and the words of my mouth be acceptable to You, Lord.* Ensure this by not talking to anything invisible, only God.

In one school of thought people think their ancestors just lose their body, but their spirit gets to remain and hang out anywhere on Earth. Nope. Not happening. Sadly, for most, many deceased people weren't even saved and had not built their spirit up to do anything useful or valuable in the Earth. If a person hasn't used their Earth journey as an opportunity to serve God and mankind, then why would God say, **Stay there and serve Me and mankind?**

Not happening.

If they've been an exemplary Christian, why shouldn't they get to go to their *reward* and rest in Peace?

An elder at a church I attended lost her husband, who was also an Elder. After he died, she admitted more than once that she would go about the house talking to him. She would ask him questions such, why he left her. She was an elder, yet talking to the invisible somehow gave her comfort, but it was not of God. By virtue of the fact that her husband was not "*with*" her and no longer on this plane, in this realm she was indicating to the devil what "form" of a *spirit* she was willing to accept to keep her company. This *spirit* could keep her company in the daytime and maybe at other times too. The devil will get in where he can fit in.

So, an Elder of a church was talking to *a familiar spirit*. It was familiar with her. It was familiar with the deceased; it was familiar with their life and their marriage. Her grief or idolatry of the man kept her connected to what she thought was *him*, but he has no way to be there with her. As an elder she should know that, but grief is a terrible thing. In my book, ***Season of Grief*** this is discussed at length. Also in my book, ***Fantasy Spirit Spouse*** I visit the dangers of this activity, unchecked. Yes, people must grieve, but the *spirit of grief* is a vicious demon, that if it can latch on it will not let go easily. Pray to break soul ties.

**Grief wants to latch on and drag you to death. Idolatrous Love cannot overcome death or grief. Only *agape* love is powerful enough to overcome grief, fear, death and the grave.**

> Many waters cannot quench love;
> rivers cannot sweep it away.
> If one were to give
> all the wealth of one's house for love,
> it would be utterly scorned.
>
> Song of Solomon 8:7 NIV

## Ancestral Powers

In what most humans believe is *ancestral worship*, acknowledging and respecting their dead relatives, they are really embracing, accepting, inviting the *powers* that have lorded over their ancestors beginning with the first sin in their bloodline.

If you are doing this, you are not acknowledging or welcoming *power* to overcome difficulties or bring you success or luck in life. You are not gaining *power* to conquer adversaries and have the great life that you desire to have, it is inviting the demons that pursued and overcame your ancestors, into your life! It is a renewal of evil covenants. So when you say ancestors, even ancestral powers, you really get **ancestral strongmen**, and your life will most likely go opposite to the way you expect. **The power to overcome in life comes from God and God alone, not from deceased relatives.**

# Spitting Image

*Yeah, he's his mother's child alright, looks just like her--, spitting image, chip off the old block.*

People are ever trying to identify either themselves with their biological parents or imagining where they fit in the life of their own family. Sadly, many do not know their biological parents, or any parents for that matter, so they can either adopt a family, be adopted by a family, get in where they can fit in, or go through life alone or as a loner.

Some males are accused of still being attached to their mothers. Women who are ready to be married but are dating a momma's boy usually say the apron strings need to be cut.

God says something else.

> … Thus says the Lord GOD to Jerusalem: Your origin and your birth are of the land of the

Canaanites; your father was an Amorite and your mother a Hittite. Eze 16:3

Your parents cared that you were born, right? They didn't just spit you out and keep it moving. But no matter where or how you were born, your parentage somehow stays with you. Even if you have lost parents or lost track of them, their "stuff" is still and ever with you--, until you change it. The umbilical cord is still attached. No, you say the obstetrician or midwife cut it. I mean *spiritually*, your umbilical is still attached. This adds a new dimension to your being attached to your bloodline. Your bloodline will be identified by your DNA. Ancestral powers will locate you, if you are not saved, and covered by the Spirit of Christ and the Blood of Jesus.

Even if you are saved in your natural family and you think you are or are really *different* from your sibs, you are still subject to bloodline stuff. Wouldn't it be better if you all acknowledged it and fought against it **together**? Don't point fingers, your family's foundation and altar might be jacked. If one of you is susceptible to the family altar's evil and lives a messed-up life, it may be that they don't have the resistance or spiritual strength that you have, or the Grace--, thank You, Lord--, what humans call *luck*. It could be that your little brother or sister was sold out by an ancestor, and you were not.

For example, when your mother was pregnant, what if she and/or your dad made a spiritual deal, thinking they were talking to God, but they were making a deal with the devil, and you were the tradeoff. So sorry if that happened to you. God is always with you. If within a family only one is saved, that saved one may have to go *through* spiritually for the rest of the family. One can do much good. Look at Jesus; He said we could do greater things than even He did.

Your *blood* will find you out, it will locate you. Your life could be the spitting image of your parent's life, good or bad. And if it was a bad life, then do something about it. Get saved and repent of **ancestral worship** *for starters*.

## Don't Set the Table

When you don't say a proper goodbye when someone dies, it's like when your computer crashes, sometimes you can't retrieve that data or that computer is never right again. Spend your time well and wisely with your loved ones. Don't take them for granted, but don't try to make up for it when they die by exalting them to some type of celebrity status.

Many cultures think it's respectful to set a place at the table for the deceased. A Jamaican friend of mine did this regularly. Don't do this.

There are festivals and holidays to commemorate the dead all over the world as we have mentioned earlier. If we haven't gotten the clue that eating food in the dream is a problem because at night the body is asleep and we don't eat in our sleep, then in death, all the more, food is not needed or eaten. Eating in the dream is a *no-no*. Eating while dead is impossible.

Jacob, in reverence to God, (Genesis 35:14), poured a drink libation. Worldwide, people sacrificed to their idol *gods* in this way. All the ancients poured out drink libations, Egyptians, Romans, Greeks, Africans, Buddhists, Nepalese, Indians, those in the Americas, Shamans in Alaska, and so on. Food and drink offerings, even if they are intended for the dead, end up as sacrifices to idols and demons.

Remember, the traditions of man do not change the Laws of God. The traditions of man debase and make the Word of God to none effect. (Mark 7:13). Even if everyone is doing it and they all took a vote on it, sill it is only what God says that stands.

People who think they are talking to their dead spouse, ancestors, and think they are getting knowledge, wisdom, instruction, approval and assistance. Those are not their dead relatives; the dead know nothing. Those are *familiar spirits* they are talking to and listening to.

People get excited when **their** *familiar spirit* is a deceased celebrity or impersonating one. Folks, the devil will try anything, and if you bite, that's what he will go with. People *channel* spirits, such as St. Germain, and others, and call them their *spirit guide*. A *lying spirit* will answer to anything; it's a *lying spirit*. It lies. This is no different than the witch at Endor summoning up dead Samuel for Saul.

A *familiar spirit* impersonated dead Samuel to trick Saul. Masquerades and impersonations by demons has not changed.

# Household Wickedness

Household wickedness is really wicked. Most of the time they don't even know they are being used by the devil. Anyone can be used of the devil for a moment, long term or permanently, unfortunately.

We all need spiritual immunity from the devil.

**Power Prayer Points:**
Lord, expose everyone in my household and inner circle partnering with darkness against me, in Jesus' Name.

Lord, I declare total war against all household wickedness now, in the Name of Jesus.

Lord of Hosts, contend with those that contend with me, in the Name of Jesus.

The counsel of household wickedness will not stand or come to pass, in the Name of Jesus.

My persecutors shall stumble, and not overcome me. They shall be greatly ashamed and will not prosper. Lord, send them into eternal discombobulation, in the Name of Jesus.

Lord, break the power of household wickedness over my life permanently, in the Name of Jesus.

Any evil marine throne, die, crumble into desolation, in the Name of Jesus.

Any evil judgment waiting for an appointed time to attack or destroy me, backfire, Lord, never leave me unguarded by your Mighty Angels, in the Name of Jesus.

Councils against me, scatter, in the Name of Jesus.

Council meetings against me, fail to convene; receive Holy Ghost Fire, in the Name of Jesus.

Every evil serpent in my life, receive Fire and be devoured by the Serpent of the Lord, in the Name of Jesus.

Any evil mind planning evil against me, scatter into perpetual confusion, in the Name of Jesus.

Any evil womb gestating evil to use against me, abort, abort, in the Name of Jesus.

Anyone or any problem in my life on a *Hari Kari* mission, die alone, in the Name of Jesus.

Spirits of my parents living inside me, come out and die, in the Name of Jesus.

Witchcraft assignments, expire, in the Name of Jesus.

**Any** weapon of destruction in the hand of my enemies, backfire, in the Name of Jesus.

Planned shame and reproach, go back to sender, in Jesus' Name.

I take back all that my ancestors lost to the devil, in the Name of Jesus.

Blood of Jesus, conquer all that is unconquered in my life, in the Name of Jesus.

Lord, synchronize my destiny clock, reset my destiny clock, purge my calendar of evil events and bring my original destiny about, in the Name of Jesus. Amen.

## *Familiar Spirits*

**Ancestral powers** are evil entities in charge of a family. They follow the family they are assigned to for generations. *Familiar spirits* are **ancestral powers**. Many times they claim to be the *spirit of the dead* within a family. This is the why of the stern warning in this book. **Ancestral powers** are **NOT** your ancestors; they are demons. They will pretend to be your grandma, grandpa, anyone that you miss, trust and would normally listen to. Everyone is assigned a guardian angel at birth; a family has one or more familial *familiar spirits* that have been there since forever. There are all kinds of spiritual influences in every life.

*Familiar spirits* are attached to a family, a tribe, a group, a neighborhood, a territory. They've been with them for years. Why do the same things keep happening in your family year after year, generation after generation? Those things that seem to automatically happen--, *familiar spirits* are responsible for the repeats, *three-peats*. Like texting on your smart phone you start a word and your phone either finishes the word for you or suggests the words for you to use in that sentence or text – that's what *familiar spirits* do.

When I wake up in the morning to look at the time on my cell phone clock it has two other suggestions for me to either text the person that I text the most often, or that I text every morning, and then a suggestion to call someone else. This is based on my patterns. UGH! I hate that! *Familiar spirits* are like that; they study you and suggest things to you that would most likely be damaging, deleterious, destructive, or devastating. But you don't realize that that is what is happening unless you are walking by the Spirit. You will think **you** thought of the idea, or this is what my family USUALLY does, or you will think dearly departed *Grandma* suggested this idea to you.

This is why we **must** learn the Voice of God.

The famous country feud of the Hatfield's and the McCoy's--, most likely *familiar spirits* were responsible for keeping that feud going for generations. Neither the Hatfield's nor the McCoy's remembered what they were originally fighting about, they just were influenced to keep the feud going.

*Familiar spirits* are responsible for the fight that you and your spouse are having that is still simmering into its $2^{nd}$ week. Neither of you really want to fight, and neither of you remember what started the fight. Demons do that, too.

## As A Man Thinketh

As a man thinketh, so is he. *Familiar spirits* influence **thinking**. If your thinking can be impacted, then your actions can be affected. When your actions please God that's a good thing. When they don't, the devil is rejoicing. So everyone in your family thinks a certain way, that's *familiar spirits* at work.

Everyone in your enclave thinks a certain way – let's say you're all racists and hate--- whatever??? That's *familiar spirit* work. You're a blue state or a red state – that's the work of *familiar spirits*.

*Familiar spirits* sponsor events that FORCE people to think a certain way, generation after generation. If they can control the thinking, they can control the actions. Actions either allow or disallow other *spirits* from coming into a person's life/neighborhood or area. If the people keep doing what the *familiar spirit* desires over and again, it's like re-electing a politician for life and then again for another lifetime, and so on. You will get the same laws, the same policies and the same results. It's a stronghold.

Deliverance is needed to change this.

*Familiar spirits* work to keep people in negative patterns, specifically in sin. When a person is defiled or in sin they are compromised for the purposes of the devil. The devil can get in and do pretty much anything he wants with an unsaved, sinner. He actually can deal treacherously with a saved but sinning person. This is why you can't get saved and then do whatever you want thinking you've done everything, spiritually speaking that you should do in life.

Selfishly, the *familiar spirit* just wants somewhere to hang out that's not HELL, but it serves the devil's purposes, so there's that.

Okay, so you are saved and NOT a sinner. Praise God! So a *familiar* or *monitoring spirit* who is allowed into your space is like a spiritual spy and can report on you without you even being aware that it is happening.

**Power Prayer Points**:

Lord, I terminate the operations of *familiar spirits* in my life, in the Name of Jesus. I declare that I am separated from my ancestry, territory of my birth and every *familiar spirit* attempting to manipulate me to reconnect me to negative ancestry patterns from my family of birth.

Every evil programmed into the Triangular Powers at my date of birth, or any other cyclic calendar date against me, be nullified, cancelled and done away with, in the Name of Jesus. Amen.

Praise God if you are discerning His voice, and not listening to *familiar spirits*. But the unsaved members of your family may not be in that same league. There could be saved people in your family who are carnal, or selfish, or bullies. Jealous bullies are especially susceptible to strongman influence.

# Strongmen

Strongmen are powers assigned to family lines to steal, kill, and destroy. I've heard some describe the strongman as a person, and yes in a sense that is true, but the *power* that the jealous person who is a bully who doesn't mind scorching the Earth against his/her own family is also called the *strongman*. The strongman mans the gate(s) of a family, or certainly tries to do so, therefore the person can also be called a gatekeeper. In the OT, elders sat at the gate. The gatekeeper of a family is not necessarily the eldest, it could be anyone, including the youngest--, the jealous, bitter, petty, selfish, insecure, evil one, even if it's the youngest.

Once sin was committed and evil covenant was forged. A strongman was assigned to a family line. Their job is to **perpetuate the evil covenant** that great-great Somebody, or even *you* made. Strongmen are powers, they are *spirits*, they not only do not die, they also do not sleep. So even if you are wishing your life was better than it is, without Jesus Christ and spiritual weapons, you might as well sit down.

***Ancestral powers*** represent the strongman **power** assigned against the family line. Strongmen are not just invisible forces – strongmen (hence the word *men*), strongwomen affect HUMANS who do their work for them in the natural. What do I mean? In the natural, strongmen are people, as I just explained.

We celebrate strongmen in weightlifting competitions, but it is nothing to celebrate, spiritually speaking.

Who is the naysayer, the opposition, the critic in your family? *Strongman spirit* is influencing your sibling to be a jerk toward you. A brother is born for adversity. A family strongman could be a close relative—it could be anyone who has access to you.

This is one of the reasons I do not like competitions and competition shows. It pits people against each other, and how do you turn that off? There is a *competitive spirit* and an **extreme** *competition spirit*. It's weird that people in a cooking competition make "friends," --, I'll say fake friends with the other competitors, but they also want to win. In order to win the other competitors must lose. How do you balance that, or do you *ever* balance that? My solution is **not** to give everyone a trophy, as in T-Ball, but let everyone **win** *something*.

You may think of the child whose big sister has a birthday, so the little brother also gets a gift. That is when we are dealing with little kids. I'm talking about big people who should be able to reason better than that at this point in their life. But they can't, or don't. In this cooking show for example, if the prize is $20,000, the first person eliminated still WINS something because they came, they stressed, they sweated and they cooked. The first to "lose," wins $2000., the next loser wins $3000.

The third wins $5000 and the grand prize winner gets $10,000. To go home with nothing is humiliating and no matter what they say in their exit interview that has to hurt. Going home with nothing says their time, energy, cooking and life is worth nothing. And that is not true; every life is worth something. Everyone's time is valuable.

Do you think the celebrity host of that cooking show would agree to go home with nothing for their time? No. And all they did was talk and eat cake.

So, as a competitor in that competition, family life is simulated for the time period of the recording of that show. I want to win and be the best, but I want the other person(s) to win too. The petty, jealous family strongman is deceitful in public, but honest to him- or herself, and horrible to the rest of the family. They want to win; they *only* want themselves to win, and they don't think there is enough winning for anyone else in the entire family. **Crabs in a basket.**

# Monitoring Spirits

The powers assigned to monitor a family lineage are called *monitoring spirits*. They watch and report to other *spirits*, rulers and principalities who have authority to **act** in a family's life.

There was a TV commercial where the dentist and assistant let the patient know that he had a cavity and then they went to lunch. They did nothing about the cavity stating that they were just monitors.

A red-light camera might take a pic of you as you run a traffic light, but it doesn't come after you with blue lights to write you a ticket. But you will get one. The enforcing arm of the government has that responsibility. If you run a toll plaza, you get a bill/ticket in the mail.

People who feel as though they are being watched could be monitored in the spirit and they feel as though they are being followed or observed. In some countries, they say they have a *follow-follow spirit*.

**Power Prayer Points:**

Lord, blind the eyes of every *monitoring spirit* assigned to monitor my destiny, in the Name of Jesus.

Lord, shatter every demonic mirror used to monitor my life and destiny, in Jesus' Name.

# Enforcers

Another branch of *ancestral powers* are the powers assigned to **execute** punishment on cursed families. Families who have made evil covenants with the devil, knowingly or unknowingly are cursed. These types of evil covenants and deals are made by people who are greedy, think they are wiser than others, want revenge or are desperate. Having an evil covenant in place gives legal right for this demon to be in your family's life making things difficult for individuals and the entire family.

Strongmen are present to ensure that that covenant is not broken, and terms and conditions of the evil covenant are met. So they enforce curses in the family and set boundaries and limitations for that family.

Their job is to keep them down, hold them back, harm them, hurt them. Why? Because these demons feel they have a legal right to something from this family that they are not getting and like the mafioso or a gang, they don't just send a colorful statement in the mail requesting it, they send a spiritual Guido to do something bad to that family. This never stops until you stop it. We can't deliver ourselves from this kind of evil. ONLY the Blood of Jesus. Only Jesus.

Enforcing strongmen visit those violating a covenant. If your great-great grandpa agreed that the men in the family would only marry witches, a strong *spirit* is sent to that family to break up marriages to non-witches or to make sure the men in that family don't marry anyone who is not a witch.

This may sound far-fetched, but it you look at the patterns in the families that you know, you will see that I'm not making this up.

# Family Captivity

*Ancestral powers* are also the *spirits* behind collective family captivity. The whole family is captive because great-great Somebody in your bloodline made a deal knowingly or unknowingly with the devil or at one of the devil's franchises. It could be that nobody in a family finishes high school, goes to college, or has a happy marriage. It could be that the family only has female children or that those children are promised to the dark world. People, this is as bad as the fairy tales we learned as kids showed us, but we were then told, Psych! That's not even true, but it is.

One sinner destroys much good. Has one person put your whole family in captivity--, sold you *all* out? How can that be? Is it because your family is not saved and has no spiritual defense? Great-great Somebody wasn't great at all; they were horrible.

# Tormentors

***Ancestral powers*** promote torment in your life. They know you by your bloodline, no matter where you are and how far you get away from your birth people, they seem to find you. They are bloodline demons; they are in your blood, so to speak.

> And his lord was wroth, and delivered him to the tormentors, till he should pay all that was due unto him.(Matt 18:34)

The torment comes because the enforcers say that you are not keeping up your end of the evil covenant and you need to be scared into compliance. (Or something like that.) Weird stuff happening in your house? Sounds? Voices? Seeing shadows, movements? This is rather subjective; torment is custom made; whatever you are afraid of, whatever irks or torments you, that's what they will try to bring.

A human being could be enticed to be your tormentor, such as your spouse who is getting on your last nerve. Your child who won't go to school or stays out nights worries you beyond worry. Your friends, a relative, and so on. Usually it is someone who lives in the house with you to bring you the most annoyance, grief, or fear. It's not the person paying you back for anything you did to them; you could have done nothing to your assigned tormentor, they are just assigned and are either on remote or are just an evil person. Stay out of sin. When you sin you lose your position and authority in the Lord and become captive. Unforgiveness is a sin that brings mega torment. It probably captures more souls than a few. Fear has torment as well. So, fear not.

> There is no fear in love; but perfect love casts out fear, because **fear involves torment**. (1 John 4:18)

# Killers & Destroyers

*Ancestral powers* are assigned to afflict a family, and there are two kinds of evil arrows, arrows of affliction and arrows of death. The devil is still working his three channels: Steal, Kill & Destroy. We really kick up a fuss when something is stolen from us, so you can imagine how bad it would be to be dialed into the other two devil channels.

**Lord, help us. Amen.**

To avoid being attacked by the devil, there is a way to break an evil covenant. We need Jesus Christ, and we need to know how to break an evil covenant while being spiritually protected before, during and after breaking it. Pay attention to this book and also other books that tell you how to be delivered and set free. Read your Bible and pray.

I am very suspicious of suspicious happenings, especially deaths. Everything is not ID Discovery; some mysterious deaths are *spiritual*. To be set free, and for your physical protection certain covenants need to be **broken**, and not just violated.

Be saved. Get saved. Be Spirit-filled. Repent of every known and unknown sin; repent of everything. Repent down your bloodline to Adam & Eve on both sides. Plead for Mercy, plead the Blood of Jesus. **Break every evil covenant** that could possibly be in effect in your life and your family's collective life. **Break, reverse and dismantle every curse**, spell, incantation, hex, vex, sorcery in your family line. The evil covenant makes the curse possible, so don't skip steps. **Break every family bondage and yoke**, following the correct protocol. **Reverse all evil judgments against you and your family.**

If you are not saved, doing any of this won't work and it could make your situation worse. Follow the steps.

*Ancestral power*, which by now you know is NOT a good thing and nothing you want to invite into your life or your family's life or worship. It is not *for* you it is **against** you. It's job is to maintain the curse by any means necessary. If the family defaults on the evil covenant, these entities proclaim judgment and then if you are not in Christ, they have their way against you. All because of some covenant that you probably don't know anything about that your ancestors agreed to, knowingly or unknowingly.

No weapon that is formed against thee shall prosper; and every tongue (that) shall rise against thee in judgment thou shalt condemn.

(Isaiah 54:17)

Great-great *Somebody* in your family formed this weapon and you, like having to disarm a bomb have to dismantle it before worse things happen in your bloodline.

*Ancestral powers* maintain sicknesses and diseases in families, such as diabetes, cancer, or insanity, for example. Haven't you had enough?

Most of the communications of ancestral strongmen to a person is via the dream. **IT IS WHY IT IS SO CRUCIAL FOR YOU TO KNOW WHAT EVERY DREAM MEANS**, Biblically. It's so you can know what they are doing and pray accordingly.

When you wake up in the morning, you see marks on your body, you have almost escaped captivity, then you get body incisions to renew the evil blood covenant.

- Father, I cancel every evil pronouncement against my life, by Fire, in the Name of Jesus.
- Anyone pronouncing sentences upon my life or members of my family, I resist you and by the Blood of Jesus, I reverse all evil judgments against me, in the Name of Jesus.
- Every evil strongman, Die, die, die, in Jesus' Name.

# Guardian Angel vs. Guardian Demon

When you are born you are assigned a guardian angel. In your life, if you choose to do wrong repeatedly, go to wrong places to sin, sin, sin, your guardian angel will depart, and you will be assigned a guardian demon. The guardian demon leads you into evil and encourages you to sin and become and remain **captive**.

A *guardian demon* is also a form of *spirit spouse*. Essentially, you're captive if you have a guardian demon, like a prison guard.

## I've Met A Few

I've met a few strongmen-- in my dreams. I seem to see at least one every week or so now. Mine look like fair complected, round headed people, or I'm seeing the same one over and over in different outfits.

They look most like the people in my mother's side of the family, whom I've never met, because they were deceased before I was born. There were a couple that looked like people on my father's side that I also never met because they were already dead before I was born.

I've heard it said that whichever side of the family they look the most like that's the foundation you need to be praying against and getting corrected, foremost.

This is one of the reasons I study and teach and share along these lines. Ancestral stuff!

## Gates & Gatekeepers

God has given us great promises, precious promises. Jesus came and died for us to have the promises that God has provided for us so, why don't we have them? Jesus came that we may have life, and we can have it more abundantly, (John 10:10).

My God shall supply all your needs according to his riches in glory, (2 Peter 1:3) and we know that God is rich. He owns the cattle on 1000 hills; all the silver and the gold are His. Some of us may be wondering where's ours? God is not a man that He should lie, or the son of man that he should repent, so where, and when does all of this *start*?

The Word says that those who know their God will be strong and do exploits, (Daniel 11:32). When does this start? I would like to do some exploits, but sometimes you need provision, means, sometimes you need connections to do some of the things that the

Lord has put in your heart to do, such as start a business, start a family, continue or finish your career.

We need open doors for this. We need open gates (open doors). Why don't we have the promises yet? Is it because of sin? Possibly. So, we will need to repent.

Is it because of evil? Probably. The devil likes to put blockages, barriers, roadblocks, stumbling blocks in our way.

Is it because of sabotage? The devil has evil human agents in the Earth who will gladly sabotage you for no reason other than, you're cute, they don't like you, or they're jealous of what they *think* you have--, or they just want to; they like mischief.

I've known people who want the house you have; they want the family you have. And this is not just TV movies. Many evil people love sabotage.

> For a great door and effectual door is opened unto me, but there are many adversaries, (1Corinthians 16:9).

There are *people* standing at these doors or at these gates, trying to hold the people of God back or block them from getting what's inside, or getting through the gates.

It's kind of like seeing a gated community with beautiful houses inside. You want to go in, but you can't because there is a gate, or there's a gate and a gatekeeper. Or there's a gate and there is an electronic thing on the wall that you can't get past because you don't know the code. There's an electronic gatekeeper.

Gates can keep things in, they can keep things out, or they can do both.

The word, *gate* is mentioned in the Bible 262 times. The word, *gates* is mentioned 107 times in the Bible. That is a whole lot of times, so gates must be pretty important. Gates protect things and people in times of war. They would have a gate and fortressed walls all around to keep their people inside safe and to keep marauding tribes out.

In the Bible, the sick, the lame, and the lepers were to be *outside* of the gate of the city. They couldn't come in except to go and show the priest that they were clean and disease free. If cleared by the priest, they would be allowed back among the community again.

We're talking about spiritual gates now, not just natural gates. Spiritual gates may have been erected in the spirit for our protection.

But if the devil has built a gate, it's an evil gate. It's to keep something from us that God has already given us, that God has promised us, something that belongs to us, to our inheritance, or to our peace.

The devil wants to keep blessings from us. He wants to keep us in lack. He wants to keep us miserable, dissatisfied with God. Satan would want to lead us into doubt, so we doubt God. And then after the trauma of doubting God and being disappointed with God, that's when he would probably pounce and try to bring a temptation to sin to try to hook us into an evil covenant and more or prolonged captivity.

# The Gates of Your Life

God has all these things that are stored for us in Heaven. There's a heavenly treasury, but we won't need money in Heaven. There's even a beautiful mansion for us in Heaven. But wouldn't some of us like a very nice house to live in, now? There are some people who don't even have houses at all. We pray that the Lord will soon give them a home.

Some of us want to live in a way that will be attractive to sinners so that we will not look like we're lost, defeated, and downtrodden ourselves. Else why would they want to come into the Kingdom of God? It is part of our witness. This is part of why the devil wants to keep us from things and things from us. And he's not playing, so we need to make sure we're not playing.

Christ died so we can have these things--, nice things. Why don't we have them?

We will ask for them today in Jesus Name. Yes, we are.

Some Christians are just eking out a living. Saints of God, we need to look good to sinners that we want to draw into the Kingdom. We need to not look bad to sinners, so they don't mock us.

The gates of your life are your career gates, your education gates, gates of your job, but they may not even be open to you. You might be working a job, but you may feel like you had to force your way in there. The gates aren't open to you if you're struggling, miserable, not getting promotions, raises, or enjoying the job. You're in it, but barely in it.

Look at God.

We're gonna ask today. We're gonna open some gates, in the Name of Jesus.

Especially if you're worried about just hanging on to your job or your career just by a thread. You just feel like it's stagnated, or you feel like you almost get the promotion and then Johnny, or Susie or somebody gets it ahead of you every time for whatever reason.

We should be walking in divine favor. There is a gate of favor. There is a Gate of Divine Favor and there's no reason why it shouldn't be open to us. There's no reason why we can't ask God for it, in the Name of Jesus, and Amen to that.

Some people look like they're not even trying. but it looks like things are so easy for them. Maybe their *doors* are open, maybe their gates are open. You've heard the term, the doors of opportunity. Maybe they're opening for these people. Well, they're gonna open for the people of God today, because we're going to pray to open these gates and doors, and entrances.

God has given us all of these precious promises. So the barricades should not be keeping us out.

*The devil.* Ugh!, him again?

Beyond these gates, as I said, there's divine favor, there's success, there's fulfillment, career, there's ministry, purpose, destiny, family. There are all kinds of things. Once you get through these gates, your faith will ramp up a few notches in the Lord. No one will ever be able to talk you out of God again. You will see that God is faithful and He is true.

You know the inheritance from Abraham? You are the seed of Abraham. You know what you're supposed to be having. Within those gates is your inheritance. We'll start with you being the seed of Abraham, Amen. And myself, the seed of Abraham.

Joshua was bringing the people out and they needed to get into Jericho, but they couldn't get in by the gate(s). Remember, they had to walk around the city. They had walked around the walls of Jericho the sixth time and the seventh time with a mighty shout, and praise and worship in the walls came tumbling down so they could get in. They had to do this because the **inheritance** was in there. By inheritance, I mean what the Lord had promised them. The land that He promised them. The precious promises that the Lord has promised you--, you will have to open some gates. It is your responsibility to know if your gates aren't open, and to ask that they be opened.

Ancestral powers are ancestral strongmen. Strongmen man the gates where your inheritance, your promises, success and things you need for your life and godliness are. We will have to bind the strongman, not worship him. We have to fire the strongman and get the gates open so we can live the abundant life that Jesus came and died for us to have.

*Gates* are mentioned 369 times in the Bible and are highly recognized in the Spirit.

The thief does not come in through the gate or the door, but he comes in through some other way. We are not thieves, so we must come through that gate.

In the natural, evil human agents are the evil gatekeepers. There are evil gatekeepers all over--, some may be in your family. Don't become a hater; we don't war with flesh and blood. Here, we deal in the Spirit, but there's no reason for you not to open your eyes and see what you need to see.

# Possess the Gates

God made His covenant with Abraham in Genesis 22:17, regarding Abraham's *children's* children, and their inheritance. It says. ***Thy seed shall possess the gates of their enemies.*** When you take the gate of an enemy you've won the battle, you've won the victory and the spoils.

In Genesis 24:60, there was a promise made that we were going to possess the gates of those people that hate us--, again, the gates of the enemy. We're will possess their gates. We are Abraham's *children's* children--, that's us. Should it have taken us all this time to understand what was intended in Genesis?

There are gates. There are spiritual gates. And we have to open them.

**God** also has gatekeepers. We have heard more talk of the Pearly Gates than probably any other Gate in the Bible. The Pearly gates are spiritual gates that John the

Divine saw and wrote about in the Book of the Revelation.

In Jerusalem there were seven natural gates clockwise and by their current names: the Damascus Gate; Herod's Gate; Lions' Gate; Golden Gate; Dung Gate; Zion Gate; and Jaffa Gate. God has Gates, and He has good gatekeepers. They're the angels of God, and at His directive, they open doors (gates) that no man can shut, and they can close doors that no man can open. They stand guard at places where we can or can't go in. For example, the cherubim with the flaming sword guarding Eden after Adam and Eve were evicted.

Today we will ask the Lord to open gates that no man can shut against us. No strong man, no evil man, no spiritual wickedness can shut these gates against us, again.

In opposition, the enemy has erected evil gates in the spirit, and they are guarded by evil gatekeepers, who are guarding these gates, and they are wicked ancestral powers; they are demons, or they *empower* the evil, human strongmen. These evil human agents are within families, and they are wishing and praying for and blocking the goodness that God has for the people of God.

Why do they do it?

Maybe to feel powerful. Maybe they think the Devil will reward them. Maybe they're just evil and are having fun. Feet that be quick to run to mischief are people who enjoy doing evil. Maybe they are fully captive and programmed, and cannot help themselves.

An evil gatekeeper is a strongman, and he is guarding a place such as a gate where either God has a lot of good stuff in there for you, or it could be stuff that the devil has stolen from you already. The Strongman has got it on lockdown.

To get what's inside, we must spoil the strongman, right? Mark 3:27 says you can't enter into a strongman's house and take his goods, unless you first bind the strongman.

The devil has human agents, blockers who are working with or possessed by demons, and they act as the evil gatekeepers.

You wonder why your life is not going well. Could be somebody in your nuclear family--, or a relative, such as a cousin--, I wouldn't put anything past pretty much anybody these days. As I said, we don't know what lengths people will go to, to do the evil they want to do until they go to those lengths.

The strongman is the demon in the spirit, and it empowers the *family strongman* in the natural. The strongman/strongwoman is a person. It is a human. It is an evil human agent in the Earth. And there are, let's say, evil city, country, family, national even international gatekeepers and they they're there to make sure that nobody reaches their God-given destiny.

Moreover the spirit lifted me up and brought me unto the east gate of the Lord's House, which looked eastward, and behold, at the door of the gate 5 and 20 men, among whom I saw Jazaniah the son of Azur, and Pelatiah the son of Binaya.
The princes of the people. (Ezekiel 11:1)

Princes of the people are respected people.

> Then said he unto me, Son of man, these *are* the men that devise mischief, and give wicked counsel in this city Which say, *It is* not near; let us build houses: this *city is* the caldron, and we *be* the flesh. (Ezekiel 11:2-4)

> Therefore prophesy against them. Prophesy oh son of man. (Ezekiel 11:4)

And the story goes on in verse 13 where Ezekiel did prophesy and Pelatiah the son of Benaniah dropped dead and that astonished Ezekiel.

> And it came to pass, when I prophesied, that Pelatiah the son of Benaiah died. Then fell I down upon my face, and cried with a loud voice, and said, Ah Lord GOD! wilt thou make a full end of the remnant of Israel? (Eze 11:13)

There are gates and there are evil men at the gates, in the natural in those times, and also in the Spirit, now.

These people at this gate, which is the position of power, a position of authority where they were devising evil for the city. There are 25 of them. So they have pretty much decided they were running things. They are confident, more than likely charged demonically. They are empowered demonically to think up evil things. We hear them say that this place is the cauldron--, that's a pot. And they devise wickedness in this pot. Witches and wizards cook up things in pots.

There are demonic, household strongmen in a family. You can know who they are by the stuff that comes out of their mouth. They make declarations such as *over their dead body Or, who do you think you are? You think you're so much. That's not gonna happen for you. Oh, you're not gonna be more successful than I am,* or *Not if I have anything to say about it.*

Yeah, that's who they are. They're telling you who they are. You may laugh and chuckle and think you're saying nothing. But if they're demonically charged, if they're demonically networked, if they're demonically empowered, and you do nothing, they could have their way over you, unless by God's Grace and Mercy, He just doesn't let anything happen to you.

But if you decide you don't want to pray, you're not going to do anything about it--, you don't believe it; you don't believe in it that may be your downfall. Witchcraft is very powerful unopposed; I keep telling you. So if you have this strongman/strongwoman in your family working unopposed, what they're saying to you might actually come to pass.

This person could block your whole family from their future, their destiny, their inheritance, purpose, and successes in their evil jealousy.

# Prophesy

Ezekiel, son of man. Prophesy, prophesy.

When you stand and pray, you prophesy. And I'm not saying to proclaim that a person drops dead like Benaiah, I'm just saying prophesy so the evil that this person wants to come to pass over your life does not come to pass, in the Name of Jesus.

Prophesy. Say, *I bind and dislodge all household strongmen, in the Name of Jesus.*

Once bound, you will see a difference in your whole family. You'll see a difference in your life. You'll begin to see breakthroughs in your family., and in your own life.

There are family gates, country gates, county gates, town gates, community gates, national gates, life gates through which are individual blessings for you.

Family gates, through which there's your family blessings, and destiny. God sees your family as a *bloodline*. God has a purpose for your bloodline. For you individually, for the people in your family--, individually, yes-- but also for your bloodline. You are responsible to pray about both. Do your part in your family. Pray, walk upright before the Lord. Stay in the Word. Keep your spiritual eyes open, see what's going on, and deal with it in the Spirit.

Your whole family is not smart for nothing. You're not creative and innovative for nothing. You're not just cute for nothing. There's a purpose in all of this for your whole family.

Why isn't that stuff that you've been prophesied about come to pass yet? Because your life has gates. In life there are gates that you have to go through. And if you do, you'll be a force to be reckoned with.

The devil hates you anyway. So he puts up blockages, including gates and evil gatekeepers, to keep you from going through the channels and the blessings in the path that you're supposed to be on. But you have the responsibility to bind all these evil gatekeepers in your life in order to go through the gates of your life.

You may not remember back that far, but as a toddler, if you have a toddler or have seen one fenced in by a baby gate – oh my! What they won't do to get out of that corral you created. You need to be that determined!

Remember what God said. Your seed will *possess* the gates of their enemies. Look at the patterns in your family. Is stuff just stagnant in your whole family? Is it in slow motion? Does it seem like nothing much is happening in your family? **You better bind the strongman.** And then we're going to ask God to *judge* that strongman.

**Here Are the Steps:**
Repent & get saved if you're not.
Be filled with the Holy Spirit.
Cover yourself with the Blood of Jesus.
Ask God for Mercy, in Jesus' Name.
Bind the strong man.
Review and do the steps to remove the **cause** for the strongman to be there in the first

place in case he/she has a legal right in your family and blocking your family's gate.

Ask God to **judge** the strong man.

And then I say, prophesy against them. Oh, Prophesy, son of man. (Ezekiel 11:4)

When the gates are unguarded, now command the gates to open. Lift up your heads, O ye Gates, (Psalm 24).

And if you say to this mountain, be thou removed and cast into the sea, it'll obey you. The mountains have ears, as well, the gates have ears. The morning has ears; that's why you can command the morning. Saints of God, the nights have ears, that's why you can command the night. And you can talk to the gate, talk to the gates, because they have ears, and they will obey you.

*Lift up ye heads, O ye Gates, so the King of Glory can come in.* The Christ in you is what the gates obey. The Christ in you is speaking, and you are speaking the Word of God, so the gate **must** obey you. It has to. You'll know that it heard because now your family starts moving forward and progressing. They become more prosperous.

Unless *you're* the problem. Are you living right before the Lord? Are you prayed up? Are you reading the Word? Are you in the will of God? Are you taking the steps to your destiny? Are you being as obedient as you can by the Holy Spirit? Amen.

You prayed and know that there are no other issues working against you. You've prayed and gotten your foundation worked out, your ancestral inheritance, any evil inheritance is cleared away. Ask the Lord to pour His salt into your foundation to heal it. You've repented, renounced, denounced all sin and broken all evil covenants? There's no active sin your life, so now you can you take it to the next level.

# What's the Name of that Gate?

Here's how you pray: first, pray for Mercy from God. You do this because you're going to be calling **judgment** on a strongman, and you better cry out for Mercy for yourself first.

You have to know the gate. What gate? What is the *name* of the gate that you can't get through? In other words, what's the blessing or what's being kept from you? That's the name of the gate that is being closed against you. A gate of the Inheritance, Gate of Business, a Gate of Favor, a Gate of Career, a Gate of Education, a Gate of Relationship, a Gate of Marriage, a Gate of Fruitfulness, a Gate of Family, a Gate of Children, a Gate of Health, and et cetera.

You're at the gate. The strongman is there; bind him.

See how *ancestral worship*, which is really worship of ancestral **powers**, is counterproductive to getting the precious promises of God for your life? Do you now see how ancestral worship is strengthening the strongman who is guarding the gate where he is keeping the precious promises that God has for your life and godliness? You have to repent, renounce and denounce that idolatrous worship and every evil covenant you have made, if you did so.

**Bind the strongman, the evil watchman at the Gate.** Once he is bound, we will ask God to **dislodge the demonic watchmen at the gate.**

**Then we're gonna talk to the gate. We're gonna say things like,** *Gate of inheritance, I command you to open, in the Name of Jesus.*

Next, we will prophesy. Be like Ezekiel, prophesy against them. Prophesy son of man, prophesy.

Now see yourself going through that gate.

And once you're through that gate, you will take what is yours. While you're taking what is yours, make prophetic declarations about what has now changed since you have access to this space, this room, this vault, this place. The strongroom holds all these goods and blessings that have been kept from you. Through that gate is tangible things and *intangible* things. Get all of what's yours--, things and stuff that belong to you, but also things like success and joy and peace. Fruitfulness.

I personally further command the Gate to stay open for me and never be closed to me again, in the Name of Jesus.

We're going to get the things that belong to us. We're gonna get the things that the enemy has had on lockdown. This is a serious extraction, requiring almost military precision. We are not going to play with this or take it lightly.

You're saved, right? This will not work if you're not saved. You need to accept Jesus as your Lord and Savior. Pause here if you need to accept Jesus first.

# & A Child Shall Lead Them

And a child shall lead them.

We have authority and responsibility to repent for our *ancestors*. Did you ever in a million years think that you could or would need to repent to God for the actions, works, deeds, and sins of your *ancestors*? If you are going to make **your** life right, if you intend that your life go right, you may have to repent for your ancestors' sins. You have to do this to heal your foundation. You cannot build the family that is to be built on your bloodline with a faulty foundation.

The fact that you can speak for your deceased ancestors should amaze you; it amazes me. We have been taught all of our lives to respect our elders and we don't dare get too casual with them. We don't dare think they have sins or have sinned, but surely, they have. We all have sinned and fallen short of the Glory of God. We are not judging, we are repenting.

People have a bucket list, the personal things that people want to do, Skydive. Travel near and far. Get married and have kids. That's the type of things many people want to *finish*. Most people think that unfinished work is physical human work –buildings, such as build the new house for your family. Finish the man cave or the dog mansion out back. Put in the swimming pool and update the kitchen to make the wife happy. They may even think that if they can get their retirement and life insurance straight, possibly set the details of their own burial that they will have completed their life's work.

But so many, too many die with undone or unfinished *spiritual* work. Unrepented for sins carry over like minutes on your cell phone service. Unused repentance is just unused.

We are standing in the future looking back – you can see so much more from certain vantage points. From above, you can see so much more. In God, in Christ--, look at all He shows us.

Time heals all things they say – well, it doesn't heal unrepented sin, BUT if we repent for our ancestors, we can undo a lot of BAD. They say one sinner destroys a lot of good. In Christ, one repenting saint of GOD can destroy a lot of bad.

Sometimes I think every night, every dream is like a video game, the adventures of captivity and every dream is a person either accepting captivity or trying to get out of captivity. dreams are the clues as to WHY you are in captivity and repenting goes a long way in getting you out, just as you might ask Mercy for yourself from a judge in the natural, the Righteous Judge will hear your cries of Mercy.

Knowing WHAT you may be repenting of is critical so you will know how to pray correctly, but also so that you and your bloodline don't fall into the same trap again. The trap of greed, lust, et cetera--, the trap that got YOU, maybe them, maybe some of them *captured*.

I think maybe in a bloodline, there was ONE who had all the fun and nothing much happened to them, well, maybe torment. Maybe a shortened life span, they were probably in captivity too, but they were either having so much fun with the bauble they traded their soul to the devil for (like a child with a new toy), that they didn't give a thought to how they were jacking up the entire bloodline to the third and the fourth generation. Generational sin goes into the 10$^{th}$ and to the 14$^{th}$ generations if a family hates God, that is an unsaved bloodline.

Is a generation 20 years, or 40 years? Either way that 200 to up to 500 years of *captivity* because of great-great Somebody who wasn't as great as he should have been. He was only great because he had a great desire for money. or he had a great desire for sex, or a great desire for revenge. These are the typical things on the devil's menu that snare men. Whenever anything is chosen on the devil's menu it comes with a side of IDOLATRY. Putting other *gods* before GOD is idolatry.

***Ancestral worship***  is not what you may think. Come out from among the tombs. Loitering among the tombs and in graveyards and cemeteries mourning and worshipping the dead is not respecting your ancestors, that's ancestral worship of demonic powers.

All power belongs to God. The power that you need to live a victorious life is in Christ Jesus, not in dead relatives.

Pay attention to your dreams, God is trying to tell you something, He is talking to you. Don't be like the man who sees himself in a mirror and goes his way forgetting what he just saw. If you are having dreams and not recording them and getting proper interpretation, this is what you are doing.

## Break Free

**To be free of ancestral powers, first** surrender your life to Jesus. I repent of all known sin, especially sins involving ***ancestral worship***. Lord, I vow to only serve You, only worship You and not elevate any other deity or serve any idol *gods,* in the Name of Jesus. Lord, please forgive me, in Jesus' Name.

Now, Lord, the entrance of Your Word brings light. Thank You for Your Word and truth in this book that has brought revelation and light to my understanding and to my life. Now it's time for spiritual warfare.

- Cancel the evil effect of evil laying on of hands upon your head by any family member, sever the transference of all evil *spirits* assigned to you at that time, in Jesus' Name.

Many of us before we got born again had evil hands laid upon our heads and we are struggling now to get out of it.

Lord, in the Name of Jesus we come boldly to the throne of Grace to obtain Grace and Mercy in this time of need. Lord, cover me with the Blood of Jesus.

Every evil strongman that is standing between me and my destiny, be dislodged and be removed, in the Name of Jesus.

I sever, and bind, the evil gatekeeper's source of power, in the Name of Jesus.

Lord, You said in Your Word that whatever is bound on Earth shall be bound in Heaven. Lord, bind the strongman, in the Name of Jesus.

Lord, I bind the strongman and I ask You to remove that evil gatekeeper, that's standing between me and what is mine, my inheritance given to me by the Lord, in the Name of Jesus.

I have been given power to tread over the works of the enemy, and I have the authority to trample on snakes and scorpions, and nothing by any means shall hurt me, in Jesus' Name.

I take authority over every evil gatekeeper standing against me, in the Name of Jesus.

I break all ties to their source of power, in the Name of Jesus. Lord, I know that all human and demonic gatekeepers who stand or sit at the gate have been bound.

**So this gate of my inheritance now has no gatekeeper because they are bound, in the Name of Jesus.**

Every evil gatekeeper that has sworn that I'll never be successful, let that gatekeeper be destroyed, in the Name of Jesus.

Every evil gatekeeper that is out to wreck my life, let that evil gatekeeper be destroyed, in the Name of Jesus.

Every evil gatekeeper who is after my life, my purpose, my Ministry, career, education, life, marriage or destiny, inheritance, business, fruitfulness, or any blessing. Whatever the name of the Gate is Lord right now, I purpose to pass through this gate, in the Name of Jesus.

I command this evil gatekeeper to be removed, to get out of the way, to depart from my path right now, in the Name of Jesus.

Every strongman or woman be removed from this gate and be dislodged, never to return. I send you to where the true Lord Jesus Christ sends you for ministry, in Jesus' Name.

All evil *spirits*, spiritual wickedness, principalities, warring angels of Heaven step in and bind you all with triple flaming fetters that cannot be undone and cast you into the Abyss for early torment, proclaiming, ***FAILED MISSION.***

Father, Righteous Judge, in the Name of Jesus, judge this wicked, evil gatekeeper that has stood in my way, judge him by Your righteous standards and by the Fire of the Holy Spirit.

Lord, God Almighty, You are a consuming Fire. Let the flaming sword of Your fury fall directly on every evil gatekeeper blocking my gate of inheritance, in the Name of Jesus.

Father, every evil gatekeeper who is the strongman in my family, let the Earth reject him or her, in Jesus' Name.

I break every link between the strongman of my family and any and all evil networks, in the Name of Jesus. I break, and I bind the power that sustains the household strongman, in the Name of Jesus.

Now that the strongman of my family has been bound and all the money gatekeepers dislodged, I speak to the gates of my inheritance, to be opened to me, in the Name of Jesus.

Every gate that my family needs to open and pass through, let it be open now, in the Name of Jesus.

Gracious Father, the gates of my life and destiny are opened, in the Name of Jesus. Every gate of prosperity and fruitfulness is open to me today, in the Name of Jesus.

Gates of Glory and honor and blessings be opened, in the Name of Jesus.

Like Ezekiel Father, I'll prophesy I will prophesy against the evil at the gates, but I will speak to the gates that they open, and stay open for me, in the Name of Jesus. (Ezekiel 26:2)

Open the gates that the righteous nation that keeps the truth may enter in. Jesus is the Truth. Starting today, starting right now, my family will be able to enter into the gates of our family's inheritance, Lord, as you have ordained.

Thank You Lord for judging the strongman.

Father, touch all the stale, dead, dry, and barren areas of my life, and resurrect them, in Jesus' Name.

Gate of Inheritance, Gate of Business, fruitfulness, family blessings--, serve this family, not evil. You do not serve the strongmen. You serve the righteous of this family. You do not serve demons, and you will never be closed to us again, in the Name of Jesus.

If you're closed to protect what is inside this room or this space or this vault, so be it. But you will never again be closed to me or my family or any righteous person in my bloodline forever, in the Name of Jesus.

By the Blood of Jesus. Holy Father grant speedy recovery of lost time, lost effort, reverse all disappointment, frustration and loss, in Jesus' Name.

Angels of God displace and disgrace the actions of all evil *spirits* involved in the blockage and blockade erected at the gate of my inheritance, in the Name of Jesus.

Heavenly Father, I take possession of everything behind this gate that belongs to me that has been held back from me, in the Name of Jesus.

Righteous Father, let there be physical manifestation in my life and in my family's life that these gates have been indeed opened and that we've been able to come in and get our inheritance and blessings that You have prepared for us, in the Name of Jesus.

I proclaim that me and my family can go visibly to the next level, from glory to glory, all the praise and all the glory and the honor is due to You, Lord, in the Name of Jesus.

Lord, thank You for hearing and honoring and answering all my prayers. I renounce, denounce and ask forgiveness for ever worshipping **ancestral powers** in error or at all.

Lord, I will not forget my transitioned loved ones, but I will not worship them, in Jesus' Name.

Thank You that the gates of my life and my family's life are now opened forever more, in the Name of Jesus.

> Therefore the gates shall be open continually. They shall not be shut day or night, (Isaiah 60:11a).

Father, thank You for restoring the years that the locust, the caterpillar, the palmer worm, the cankerworm have eaten, in the Name of Jesus. Lord, redeem the time, restore the years.

Lord, You have said in Your Word that when the thief is caught, he must repay sevenfold. I demand, in the Name of Jesus repayment of not less than sevenfold of what the enemy took from me and my family in finances, time, frustration, and other losses. Let the misery that the enemy has inflicted on us, be return to him in spades, in the Name of Jesus.

Thank You, Lord. For the restoration of my life and my family's life, in the Name of Jesus, to You be all glory, honor and praise, in the Name of Jesus, Amen. Amen.

Lord Jesus, come into my life. I accept You as my Lord and Personal Savior. I believe in my heart You died and rose from the dead to save me. Thank You, Lord for saving me, in Jesus Name, Amen.

I seal these declarations across every realm, age, era, dimension, and timeline, past present and future, to infinity. I bind up every retaliatory spirit and power and command all attacks against me because of these prayers backfire on the enemy, in the Name of Jesus.

Thank You, Lord.

**AMEN**

# Other books by this author

 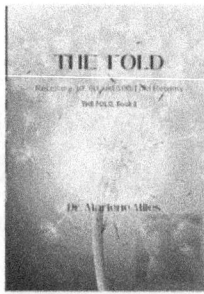 

**AK: The Adventures of the Agape Kid**

**AMONG SOME THIEVES**

**Churchzilla,** *The Wanna-Be, Supposed-to-be Bride of Christ*

**Demons Hate Questions**

**Don't Refuse Me, Lord (4 book series)**

**Evil Touch**

**The Fold (4 book series)**

- The Fold (Book 1)
- Name Your Seed (Book 2)
- The Poor Attitudes of Money (Book 3)
- Do Not Orphan Your Seed
- got HEALING? Verses for Life
- got LOVE? Verses for Life
- got money?
- How to Dental Assist
- Let Me Have A Dollar's Worth
- Man Safari, *The*
- Marriage Ed. *Rules of Engagement & Marriage*
- Made Perfect in Love
- Power Money: Nine Times the Tithe
- The Power of Wealth *(forthcoming)*
- Seasons of Grief
- Seasons of War *(forthcoming)*
- The Spirit of Poverty *(forthcoming)*
- Triangular Power *(series)*
  - Powers Above
  - SUNBLOCK
  - Do Not Swear by the Moon

**STARSTRUCK**

**Warfare Prayer Against Poverty**

**When the Devourer is Rebuked**

**The Wilderness Romance** *(3-book series)*

    ***The Social Wilderness***

    ***The Sexual Wilderness***

    ***The Spiritual Wilderness***